Practicing Mindfulness

How to Stop Overthinking, Declutter Your Mind and Get Rid of Stress

(Practice the Art of Reflection, Mindfulness & Happiness)

Bruce Popp

Published by Rob Miles

© **Bruce Popp**

All Rights Reserved

Practicing Mindfulness: How to Stop Overthinking, Declutter Your Mind and Get Rid of Stress (Practice the Art of Reflection, Mindfulness & Happiness)

ISBN 978-1-989990-89-6

All rights reserved. No part of this guide may be reproduced in any form without permission in writing from the publisher except in the case of brief quotations embodied in critical articles or reviews.

LEGAL & DISCLAIMER

The information contained in this book is not designed to replace or take the place of any form of medicine or professional medical advice. The information in this book has been provided for educational and entertainment purposes only.

The information contained in this book has been compiled from sources deemed reliable, and it is accurate to the best of the Author's knowledge; however, the Author cannot guarantee its accuracy and validity and cannot be held liable for any errors or omissions. Changes are periodically made to this book. You must consult your doctor or get professional medical advice before using any of the suggested remedies, techniques, or information in this book.

Upon using the information contained in this book, you agree to hold harmless the Author from and against any damages, costs, and expenses, including any legal fees potentially resulting from the application of any of the information provided by this guide. This disclaimer applies to any damages or injury caused by the use and application, whether directly or indirectly, of any advice or information presented, whether for breach of contract, tort, negligence, personal injury, criminal intent, or under any other cause of action.

You agree to accept all risks of using the information presented inside this book. You need to consult a professional medical practitioner in order to ensure you are both able and healthy enough to participate in this program.

Table of Contents

INTRODUCTION 1

CHAPTER 1: WHAT IS MINDFULNESS? 4

CHAPTER 2: HOW TO DO IT (JUST DO IT) 11

CHAPTER 3: INSIGHT INTO MINDFULNESS 30

CHAPTER 4: WHAT IS MINDFULNESS? 49

CHAPTER 5: WHAT IS MINDFULNESS, AND WHY SHOULD I CARE? 60

CHAPTER 6: HOW TO BE MINDFUL 80

CHAPTER 7: MINDFULNESS EXERCISES THAT INVOLVE THE BODY 96

CHAPTER 8: STARTING ON YOUR OWN 104

CHAPTER 9: DEEP BREATHING FOR STRESS RELIEF 114

CHAPTER 10: USING MINDFULNESS TO DEAL WITH ADDICTIONS 126

CHAPTER 11: MINDFULNESS MEDITATION STEP-BY-STEP 138

CHAPTER 12: WHAT IS MINDFULNESS? 146

CHAPTER 13: THE GREATEST PARTNER WE ALL HAVE 156

CHAPTER 14: WHAT IS MINDFULNESS? 169

CHAPTER 15: WHAT IS MINDFULNESS AND WHAT ARE ITS BENEFITS? 179

CHAPTER 16: MINDFULNESS USED IN OTHER ANXIETY RELATED SITUATIONS 188

CHAPTER 17: MEDITATION 194

CONCLUSION 201

Introduction

Have you ever forgotten someone's name after meeting him or her? Have you ever asked a question without listening to the answers? Do you feel like you are living your life on autopilot? Do you feel that your emotions and feelings control you and not the other way around? Are you tired of living your life in the past and having to constantly worry about the future? Do you think about work when you are at home and do you think about home when you are at work, without even realizing that you have been doing it? On a daily basis, how much time do you actually spend in the moment, rather than thinking about the future or reflecting on the past? Do you want to start living in the present? Then this is the perfect book for you.

This book will help you understand what mindfulness means and the various advantages of being mindful. Not just this, but it also includes various tips, strategies, and ideas that will help you in being mindful in your daily life. In addition, this book will teach you about mindful eating and what it means to be a mindful parenting.

Being mindful will lead to reduction in both stress and anxiety levels. Meditation and breathing techniques are quite popular in helping you achieve this and this book will teach you easy methods of doing so. By being consciously aware of your eating habits, practicing mindfulness exercises, and doing something as simple as reciting mantras, you will be well on your way to the path of achieving mindfulness.

By following the simple tips given in this book, and introducing them into your daily routine, you will definitely be more mindful. A little effort really does go a long way. So, without further ado, let's get started!

Thanks again for purchasing this book, I hope you enjoy it!

Chapter 1: What is Mindfulness?

The definition of mindfulness varies slightly depending who you ask. According to Jon Kabat-Zinn, a leading teacher of mindfulness techniques, mindfulness "means paying attention in a particular way; one purpose, in the present moment, and nonjudgmentally." Essentially, mindfulness involves cultivating an awareness of the present – it involves being an active observer of and participant in our own lives rather than letting things pass by unnoticed. It also involves paying attention to your actions and thoughts without judging them.

To give you an idea what mindfulness looks like, take the example of eating breakfast. Normally, you might sit down to breakfast at the kitchen table and browse through the morning paper as you eat. While you eat and look over the paper you may also be thinking ahead to your to-do list for the day – your mind probably isn't focused on any one thing. Rather, it flits from one thought to the next as your body operates on auto-pilot.

If you introduced mindfulness into your morning routine, breakfast might look completely different. You would sit down at the table with your breakfast placed in front of you and you would eat slowly, focusing on the details of the process. You would pay attention to the feeling of the smooth metal of your fork or spoon in your grasp and you would focus on the sensation of food passing over your tongue and down your throat. When your mind begins to wander, you would reign it in, maintaining an awareness of the physical sensations you encounter while eating.

Mindfulness can certainly take some time and practice to master, but it is by no means a difficult process. You simply have to recognize it when you begin to operate on autopilot and when your mind starts to wander so you can bring yourself back to the present moment and focus on the task at hand. Before getting into the details about how to practice mindfulness or even the benefits it provides, take a moment to read about the history of mindfulness and how it came to be part of mainstream medicine.

The History of Mindfulness

The practice of mindfulness, though it has only recently become part of mainstream medicine, originated with Buddhist monks more than 2,500 years ago. The type of mindfulness people practice today looks a little different than it did 2,500 years ago. In the time of early Buddhist monks, meditation was used to achieve both spiritual and intellectual enlightenment and it was also used to strengthen the mind and its capacity for intense concentration.

Many early religions practiced some kind of meditation or prayer that served to shift a person's thoughts away from usual preoccupations toward a greater perspective on life. Modern mindfulness also has some ties to the scriptures (Sutra) of Patanjali which date back about 5,000 years. These scriptures represent an atheistic approach to the Four Vedas – an important aspect of the Hindu religious, each representing a particular concept. The Four Vedas represent ritual; devotion through music; gaining/sharing knowledge; and removal of harmful substances or practices.

Because the Sutra of Patanjali is so old, it is unknown whether it was written by a single person or a group of persons. Though the Sutra of Patanjali is not directly mentioned in modern practices of mindfulness, some of its concepts resonate well with mindfulness techniques. For example, the Sutra urges you to "surrender to that which is beyond your power" – to accept that which you have no control over and to release it. The Sutra of Patanjali also urges readers to keep to a single principle, method or practice rather than switching between multiple methods. Discipline is required to reach your goal.

Although the principle and practice of mindfulness can be traced back thousands of years to many different cultures and religions, the modern practice of mindfulness is largely attributed to one person – Jon Kabat-Zinn. Kabat-Zinn is a professor emeritus and the former director of a clinic for stress reduction which is part of the Medical Center at the University of Massachusetts. Kabat-Zinn studied under Buddhist teachers and created a stress reduction program called Mindfulness-Based Stress Reduction. Kabat-Zinn is the founder of a medical center that focuses on mindfulness techniques in order to help people overcome stress, pain, anxiety, and illness.

Now that you understand what mindfulness is and where it comes from you can learn how this practice can impact and improve your life. In the next chapter you will receive in-depth information regarding the benefits of mindfulness for your physical and mental wellbeing.

CHAPTER 2: HOW TO DO IT (JUST DO IT)

MINDFULNESS MEDITATION: AN OVERVIEW

In this chapter we're going to look at the practice of mindfulness in more detail, with some more guided meditations for you to try. By now you should have experienced mindfulness practice at least twice, by following the guided meditations at the beginning of each of the first two chapters, and perhaps you've followed the advice and continued to take time out to practice your new-found skills throughout the day. If you have, then you should know that you are already starting to develop a new habit, which is awesome. Well done! In Chapter 3 we'll explore how to practice regularly, but for now let's look at mindfulness training in more detail.

Types of mindfulness practice

Although this book will guide you through various methods of practicing mindfulness, it's important to remember that the ultimate goal — if having a goal is even appropriate! — is to learn and develop the habit of mindfulness wherever you are and whatever you're doing. For now we'll take our 3 minute time-outs in a conscious way, and we'll do that as often as possible. But in time, becoming more aware and "paying attention to present moment experience with open curiosity and a willingness to be with what is" will become second-nature to you. With that in mind, here are three tips to help you develop the habit of everyday mindfulness, no matter where you are, or what you're doing:

Pay attention to your breathing, particularly when you are experiencing intense emotions, such as anger or joy. Notice the emotions, and then notice your breathing. Don't try to change your emotions ostensibly, simply notice them and pay close attention to your breath. How does it sound? Feel? How does it change while you are paying close attention?

Notice what sensations you are experiencing at any given point in the day. Stop and take a moment to really notice what is going on around you — sights, sounds, smells, colors, texture, the taste of the air, the emotions your surroundings are producing in you right now. Don't analyze the information you take in, just notice and enjoy the fact that you are noticing what most people allow to slip by them 99% of the time.

Tune your attention into physical sensations whenever you can. Getting into the bath – how does the water feel on your skin? Eating a meal – what effect does each mouthful have on your tongue, your lips, how does it taste? Sitting on a bus or a train, or in the car – how does the seat hold your body, where are you hot, cold, uncomfortable, tense?

Keep it simple, and start with these 3 reminders, keeping them with you throughout the day. Now let's move on to what you can expect during your more structured mindfulness practice.

What to do with your body and your mind

This is probably the most common question asked by people embarking upon any meditation program, and the answer is not as complicated as you might expect. In the next section we'll look at where you might want to carry out your planned sessions, and the variety of options shows that there really aren't any hard and fast rules for mindfulness meditation. If you prefer to be sitting, sit. If you get more out of mindfulness by going for a walk, surrounded by nature or by a busy street, then that's what you should do.

But for the planned practice, it's usually best initially to find a quiet place in your home or garden and sit comfortably where there is no tension on your body. Lying down works for some people, but there's always the danger you'll fall asleep (I know I do), and while sleep is fantastic, it's not the same as mindfulness. Eliminate distractions as far as possible – more on this later in the book. Relax your body. Relax your mind. The guided meditations will take you through various techniques for relaxing the mind and body, from the body scan technique to those which focus primarily on the breath. Don't try to force stillness if stillness is not comfortable for you. If you move, notice yourself moving and then bring your attention back to the meditation.

What you focus on will depend upon the mindfulness technique you are practicing. Mental focus exercises, like the one at the beginning of this chapter, ask that you try to remain focused on a particular object, gently bringing your mind back to the object when it starts to wander – and it will start to wander! Body focus meditations are about focusing on part of the body, perhaps where you are feeling pain or simply to put you back in touch with your physical sensations. Remember to be non-judgmental and kind to yourself. If your attention shifts, if your thoughts race away with you or you just can't get into it, there will always be another 3 minutes where you can try again.

What to expect as you start practicing

Right now you're probably wondering how long it will be before you see some benefits, right? You've invested this much time, and you've opened your mind to the possibilities of mindfulness, but really you'd like to know when the payoff comes.

Here's the bad news: you might start to feel worse before you feel better. Some people sail into mindfulness and blissfully segue into a child-like state, full of love and joy and inner calm. This might be you. Or you might begin to feel more anxious at first, more self-conscious, more stressed. Don't worry. This is a common side-effect, and it just means you're doing it right. Good news! Your body and mind simply need a little more time to adapt to this new way of experiencing the world, and you need to trust that mindfulness is worth carrying on with.

Breathing

The breath is key to mindfulness practice. Here we'll look at breathing, how to breathe, and how to pay attention to the breath. And we're going to do that with a little guided mediation. Find yourself somewhere comfortable to sit down if you're not already seated, and if you're wearing a tight belt maybe you should loosen it now. You won't need long for this exercise. Just 3 minutes.

Guided Mindful Breathing Meditation

Take a look at your watch or clock and note the time. Close your eyes. For the next 60 seconds you are going to focus on your breathing. Start by breathing in and out slowly. Let your shoulders relax. After a couple of breaths, start to hold your breath inside after inhaling, just for a few seconds. Then, begin to breathe in for a count of six, hold for a count of six, and out for a count of six. When you feel that 60 seconds has passed, open your eyes. Take a moment to stretch and shrug your shoulders a few times. Note the time again, and close your eyes. Now focus on your breath again, in for six seconds, hold for six seconds, out for six seconds. Really feel your breath entering your body, see it filling your lungs, expanding, filling you up with life. See it leaving you, taking impurities with it, expelling and dissipating into the air around you. When you feel another 60 seconds has passed, open your eyes and smile. Your mindful breathing meditation is complete.

Breathing is something we all do, all day, all the time. We are, however, largely unaware of our breathing, just as we are unaware of so many things within and outside of our bodies. Beginning to focus intentionally on our breath helps to ground us in the present moment. In this exercise you are also starting to control your breathing to a certain extent, not merely observing it, which may seem counter to the mindfulness definitions we've looked at so far. However, even while merely observing the breath you will find your mind begins to regulate your breathing, to form a pattern, and with this comes a beautiful calmness. This basic breathing meditation in fact underpins all other types of mindfulness practice, for it is always possible to bring the mind back to the breath whenever it wanders, bringing your attention gently back to your breath, noticing the inhalation and exhalation, noticing and focusing anew.

Anxiety and breathing - Overbreathing

Sometimes focusing on the breath can cause an adverse reaction, and you find yourself becoming anxious, perhaps breathing too shallowly, or too deeply, or too quickly, often called overbreathing. If this is you, don't panic — that will only make it worse. Later in this book we will look at common problems experienced during mindfulness training, but for now just know that you are doing nothing wrong. Sometimes the very act of giving our attention to something in a very focused way causes the observed action to increase or go haywire — think about a time when a friend pointed out something irritating, like music from a noisy neighbor or an unpleasant smell that you hadn't been aware of a moment ago. Once you are aware of it, it just won't go away — and it seems to get louder or worse the more you focus on it! Step back and remember to simply observe your breath non-judgmentally. And at the end of the meditation, you could gently ask yourself: What is my breath trying to tell me? More on this later.

PLANNED MEDITATION AND MINDFULNESS ON THE GO

Sitting, walking, lying down – Why you should do it your way

As we've seen, there are many ways to practice mindfulness, and not all of them involve sitting in a quiet room. For the purposes of this book, you are simply trying to find time in your day to build the habit of mindfulness into your life. You are experimenting with different types of mindfulness meditations, hopefully having fun, learning about your body and your own personal experience of the world around you. This is just the beginning. Mindfulness practice, once embedded in your life, is something you can and should continue to develop for years to come. Once you begin to notice the wonderful effects mindfulness has on your levels of stress, on how you interact with your children and loved ones, and on your overall sense of calm and happiness, I believe you will want to carry on making time to practice.

At this stage, however, it's probably a good idea to simply try out all the various different guided meditations at the beginning of each chapter, and those within some of the chapters, to find out which appeals to you the most. Don't take it too seriously. Be light, be open, have fun with it. Be adaptive. Get your kids involved, or ask a partner to help with some of the guided meditations by reading them out for you. Get to know yourself, and keep coming back to our favorite definition. Remember that mindfulness is "Paying attention to present moment experience with open curiosity and a willingness to be with what is." That's all. It's a habit that can be built in six days and one that can last a lifetime – but only if you learn to do it your way. Sitting, walking, lying down, swinging in the garden, swimming, running, standing on one leg; to music, in peace and quiet, with an audio track, to the sound of birds singing – try to incorporate the short mindfulness meditations into your life in any way you can, and in a way that makes you feel better. And don't let anyone tell you you're doing it wrong. You're not. If you're doing it, you're not doing it wrong.

3 Minute Mindfulness Meditation

Mindfully Experiencing a Regular Routine

What to do:

Think of a routine that you find yourself doing regularly, but one that you usually do "mindlessly" – without thinking about it at all. This could be, for example, cleaning the bath, putting away clean clothes, washing the car, or making a sandwich. Keep it short, as we only want to spend three minutes on this for now.

Now create an entirely new experience out of this routine chore. Notice every aspect of it, notice each minute detail. Pay attention to your actions, the movements of your hands, the muscles you use and how that feels. If your chosen task is cleaning-related, really notice the dirt, and notice it being removed. Notice colors and smells; notice the sounds you produce while completing this task. Be aware of every step and ask yourself if you enjoy it. Listen to, but do not judge, the answer.

Reflections:

This mindfulness meditation is designed to develop a sense of contentedness in the moment, even when you are performing routine – and sometimes onerous – tasks or chores. Many of us fall prey to simply waiting for a job to end, rushing through it to get to the next thing, the next thing.

Paying mindful attention to the daily activities that take up a lot of our time is a way of truly experiencing every day, not simply existing.

What next?

Try to find time to practice this short meditation a few more times today – whenever you find yourself doing something routinely, without thinking about it.

Chapter 3: Insight into Mindfulness

Life is short and uncertain and in this short and unpredictable life, we all face a lot of challenges on momentarily basis. How you react to the challenges and your success rate, as far as dealing with the challenges will have a great impact on your life.

If you fail to overcome the difficulties you face in life, you build regrets for the moments that you have failed yourself. One of the major reasons of this failure to meet your expectations for a challenge or difficulty that comes your way is that you are not present at the moment to push yourself to the point where you can combat the difficulty with your full strength and attention. Think about it;

when you don't give your job your all because you are busy thinking of how much you hate the job, how your boss frustrates you or how the business/industry is doing badly, the truth is that you are highly likely to land in more trouble with your boss and ultimately end up loathing yourself even the more. And if you are fired for nonperformance, you hate yourself even the more; how you could just not even keep a job that you distasted anyway!

On the contrary, if you are mindful at all times, you better understand the sensitivity of the situation and do something that is required to get yourself out of a difficult situation. This way, you succeed in overcoming any difficulty that life throws upon you and hence build no regrets to haunt you in life. As a result, the quality of your life improves as you start enjoying each moment of your life as it passes.

There has been a mention of the word 'mindful' in the previous text. What exactly does it mean?

Let me explain.

Understanding Mindfulness

Mindfulness is your ability to stay fully aware of each and every moment, as it passes. It's your ability to focus all your attention on the present moment and not getting overwhelmed by thinking of the past events or those that are yet to come.

We live in an uncertain world filled with an endless list of demands; we have stuff that demands our attention, our time, our finances and lots of other resources that we often have in limited supply. In our quest to cope with the endless demands of life, we operate somewhat on 'autopilot' on many aspects of our life; our brain is advanced in such a way that it only wants to make a limited number of conscious decisions every day. That's why it automates some of them so that it dedicates enough energy and attention for a limited number of thoughts/decisions. But with the endless number of things that we expose our brains to every single day, you can bet that it will selectively ignore a huge number of them. Instead, it focuses greatly on scanning for potential threats (by checking the future or past) to our survival especially given that we tend to have a negativity bias. Since the number of potential threats and regrets are many, that explains why we are chronically stressed, depressed, anxious and unhappy.

The good news is that if we channel our mental focus to our present instead of our future, which is yet to come or our past, which has is already gone, we can make better use of our time and other resources and ultimately live a happy and fulfilling life free from stress, anxiety and depression. If you're mindful, you don't worry yourself by thinking of the uncertainties that the future can bring, neither do you get lost in the events that have happened in the past, as all your attention is on the activities you are doing in the present.

When you put your focus on being aware of every moment as it unfolds, you are likely to derive a wide array of benefits some of which include:

The Benefits of Practicing Mindfulness

The benefits of practicing mindfulness are countless. Here are some of the major benefits of practicing mindfulness.

When you become completely mindful, you always focus on the activities you do in the present. This can be a great way of dealing with stress, anxiety and depression because, as we mentioned, mindlessness tends to be anchored on the future or pastp, which have a tendency of making us scared (anxious) and regret various aspects of our life.

Practicing mindfulness also increases your ability to focus on a particular task because when you are mindful, your attention is on the activity at hand. This improves your performance at work and also helps you deal with the challenges of life a lot easier than that you do when you aren't mindful. By being mindful, you achieve your goals a lot faster as your concentration levels are higher than ever.

Mindfulness also helps you improve your relationships with your loved ones. This is because being mindful helps you become more involved with your loved ones while interacting with them. When you show care and affection to your loved ones, they start liking you more which in turn strengthens your bond with them. Moreover, mindfulness helps you build new relationships because wherever you go, you are people's favorite due to your ability to stay fully present while interacting with people. No one likes being around anyone who seems to be far away mentally.

These are just a few of the 'everyday' benefits of mindfulness. Mindfulness has many scientifically proven, far reaching benefits many of which have been. For instance, it is not just about helping you to appreciate your present more and unplugging from the future or the past to fight stress; mindfulness is being used as a

stress reduction technique in various hospitals around the world.

Mindfulness can also:

Boost working memory

Enhance your cognitive flexibility

Help hasten recovery

Enhance general health

Improve your academic success

Help you cope with bullying and depression while at school

Help boost resilience

Help decrease burnout and turnover at the work place

And much, much more!

You can learn more about some of the scientific benefits of mindfulness **here**, **here** and **here**.

Now that you have learnt some of the benefits associated with practicing mindfulness, you probably are excited to get started. So, where do you start? That's what we will discuss next.

Before we get to learn how to practice mindfulness, let's briefly take a quick look at how mindfulness started and grew to what it is today i.e. a scientifically proven practice for deriving the benefits mentioned above and much more.

How Mindfulness Came Into Existence: A Brief Recap

Currently, the practice of mindfulness is linked to many religions and various secular traditions including Hinduism & Buddhism, yoga as well as non-religious meditation. This doesn't mean that mindfulness is a new found 'fad' that developed just recently to meet today's challenging demands. On the contrary, the practice of meditation dates back to several thousand years ago when people practiced mindfulness as a practice by itself or part of a larger tradition long before it came to the west. Originally, it helped those who practiced it to attain immense peace and to connect with their inner self and divine. It was a great way of being one with nature. Let me briefly specify the dates just so you understand how mindfulness has been around for ages:

In the East, the history of achieving mindfulness dates back to 1500 BC when the practice of yoga was first developed by the Hindus. One of the aims of the practice was to achieve peace of mind and spiritual enlightenment through mindfulness. Later on, an exercise named as Qi Gong was developed in Daoism around 600 BC. Buddhism also developed a breathing exercise around 535 BC to achieve mindfulness.

Although mindfulness as a practice took thousands of years in the east before it could spread to other parts of the world, it is increasingly becoming even more popular in the west than it is in the east! In just a few decades since mindfulness started spreading in the west, the world is increasingly finding new reasons why mindfulness is more than just a religious practice but a way to derive various benefits.

While mindfulness was originally popularized by religious and spiritual institutions in the east, the western practice of mindfulness (which came recently) was largely popularized by individuals (e.g. Jon Kabat-Zin through his MBSR (Mindfulness-Based Stress Reduction) program, and secular institutions (e.g. University of Massachusetts Medical School through its Center for Mindfulness). Today, mindfulness has grown to become more than just part of a religious practice but a practice that stands on itself, which is responsible for bringing a wide array of benefits **some of which we have discussed above**.

With that quick understanding of how mindfulness has come a long way, let's now discuss how to practice mindfulness in order to derive the benefits we discussed.

Cultivate Mindfulness by Practicing Mindful Breathing Meditation

The basic and one of the most effective strategies to cultivate mindfulness in your life is to practice mindfulness breathing meditation, which is a simple technique that increases your concentration as well as your ability to stay mindful at all times. In this technique, you try to focus on your breaths for a short time period, usually 5 – 10 minutes in the start on daily basis.

When you practice mindfulness breathing meditation on a regular basis, you train your mind to stay focused on one thing at a time, in this case your breath. This slowly trains you to develop a habit to concentrate on one activity at a time even when you are not meditating. The positive effects of mindfulness breathing meditation soon start to show their magic as after few weeks of practice, you become more involved in every activity you do. As a result, you take more interest in your present related activities and do things easily without overthinking much.

Here's how can you practice mindful breathing meditation to cultivate mindfulness in your life.

How to Practice Mindful Breathing Meditation

Follow these steps to practice mindful breathing meditation.

Sit in a quiet and comfortable place such as your bedroom or your backyard so you don't get disturbed when you meditate. If you don't have the time to practice it at home then make sure to find a quiet place for 5 minutes where nobody can distract you.

Once you find a quiet place, sit there in a comfortable position. Any position that you're comfortable in will work. You can kneel down, cross your legs or even sit in a chair.

Take a deep breath by inhaling in as much air as you can from your nose and exhaling as much as you can from your mouth.

Now close your eyes, start taking deep breaths from your nose and concentrate on your breaths while you breathe. You can do that by concentrating on the flow of air, as it enters from your nose into your body, passing through your throat into your lungs, swelling your lungs and then flowing back to your throat and moving out from your nostrils.

Keep concentrating on your breaths by noticing the flow of air for the next 5 minutes. As you do that, you will find yourself thinking of distracting thoughts that disrupt your concentration. It's quite normal and happens to all of us. When you wander off in thought, gently disengage yourself from your thoughts and bring your attention back to your breaths.

Keep your attention on your breaths this way for the next 5 minutes. You can set a timer on your mobile for 5 minutes so you don't get distracted when you try to keep track of time. Once you are able to concentrate on your breaths without getting distracted by your thoughts for a whole session of 5 minutes then increase the time to further increase your ability to stay mindful at all times.

Keep meditating this way on a regular basis and you will find yourself enjoying your routine life more than before. Also, you will find your stress levels decreased to a great extent.

To stop overthinking for good and become peaceful, becoming mindful of your thoughts is important. The next chapter teaches you how to do that.

Chapter 4: What is Mindfulness?

Start by doing what's necessary; then do what's possible; and suddenly you are doing the impossible.

- Francis of Assisi

The History and Origin

There are plenty of resources that can be referred to understand about origin of Mindfulness. It is redefined to establish contextual approach towards different adaptations. This concept has gained popularity amongst common mass in Western countries in correlations with psychological context. It has become an innovative approach in applied psychology that deals in treatment of various psychopathic conditions and syndromes. The majority of therapeutic implementations are used to eliminate the disorders like as anxiety, negative thoughts, depression, and compulsive disorders. These adaptations have shown significant improvements in the above complications. Its prolonged usage has shown excellent developments in terms of increased satisfactions, mental calm and positive mentality.

The ancient context of Mindfulness relates with the Buddhist philosophy as per the documented evidence in the nearest ideology based on similarity. Besides, there are various approaches that can be found in ancient classical texts of Ayurveda (the Indian system of Medicine) and Yoga. The can be considered as basic concepts in the field of meditation and relates with advanced development of mind and body to attain higher intelligence. These contexts date back to approximately 2500 years earlier than Buddha. There are no significant ideas that may establish the concept of Mindfulness as either ancient or latest practice. It can be considered as the fusion of various concepts with practical implementations in different day-to-day usage.

In short it can be best described as the practice of acceptance and observation. The most widely accepted definition of Mindfulness states; "the intentional, accepting and non-judgmental focus of one's attention on the emotions, thoughts and sensations occurring in the present moment"

Similar concepts

There are different meditative approaches in psychology and classical texts that have various similarities with concept of mindfulness. These are derived from different researches carried out in the field of psychology and holistic realms.

It is quite important for the beginners in mindfulness to go through these concepts so as to clear their doubts and avoid any confusion.

Access concentration or Flow

Mindfulness is often confused with this concept. It is described as an approach towards attaining the state with deeper concentration. It can be considered as a method where the user practices to focus on particular subject or ideology. This is a type of skill development that required you to be mindful about objectives where as mindfulness relieves you from any sort of adaptation that require concentration development.

Higher Meditation

There are various practices prevailing that are based on attaining state of higher concentration. The methodologies like Silva Mind Training that teaches higher intelligence, Transcend Meditation and others, which focus on attainment of a state of mind whereby its performance enhances manifold. These can be easily confused with meditative approach used in learning mindfulness, but the whole concept has altogether contrast dimension as it relives you from attaining state of meditative excellence. The basic idea differs in implementation of mindfulness as acceptance and the others depend on attainment of a higher zone.

Samadhi (Yoga-State of No Mind)

It is one of the most discussed concepts that have relations with concept of mindfulness to larger extent. It is attained by practicing different methods described in Yoga are quite similar to Mindfulness but its ultimate aim is to attain a positions of absolute thought or a state where the time interval between two thoughts increases infinitely. It is different on the basis of relativity as mindfulness is related to acceptance and observation where as this relates to elimination of thoughts and objectives.

Ancient & Modern Concepts

While starting in the field of mindfulness as a beginner you must understand about the Ancient and Modern context of the concept. It will be quite helpful for you to understand its approach and ideology. This basic information is needed to establish correlation among basic practices and its implementations as per your needs.

Mindfulness in ancient context

It is derived from the various meditational practices (reference: **https://en.wikipedia.org/wiki/Mindfulne ss - cite_note-FOOTNOTEZgierska2009-1**) that are described in the Buddhist Anapanasati. The concept of Mindfulness is based on the Pali term <u>Sati</u> that means mindfulness and is an important part of Buddhist meditative practices Vipassana, Satipatthana, and Anapanasati. These are important methods of Buddhist approach. The concept of Mindfulness based on these elements gained popularity from the MBSR (Mindfulness Based Stress Reduction) program evolved by Jon Kabat-Zinn.

The ancient Yoga sutras by Patanjali from India also reflect some aspects of Mindfulness in the "Ashtanng Yoga" (Eight phases of Yoga). The Yama and Niyama of these eight phases of Yoga quite resemble the basic s of Mindfulness principles as described in Anapanasati. In fact the Buddhist approach can be considered to be derived from ancient yoga concepts and principles in more focused manner. All these principles are derived from similar objectives that are mental enhancements and attaining the higher states of mind. These objectives are focused on mental well being and relaxations leading to healthy state of body and mind. Mindfulness has gained its form from these principles with a more definitive approach towards resolving ailments and improving health and performance in various aspects of life.

Mindfulness in modern context

The current practices are based on the MBSR program and rest all adaptations are coming out from implementations and improvements of these practices in much detailed applications. In modern context the concept of mindfulness is largely associated with clinical psychology and psychiatric practices. After the inception of MBSR a lot of therapeutic applications have been developed on Mindfulness for the patients suffering from various psychological disorders. These practices based on mindfulness have gained worldwide recognition for the benefits in eliminating stress, anxiety, emotional withdrawal and treatment of psychopathic conditions like as depression and other compulsive disorders.

Mindfulness is fund to be useful in managing the conditions related to emotional crisis and breakdown very effectively. The clinical researches based on the MBSR and mindfulness based techniques are acclaimed as psychological treatment modalities for different areas like as hospital, prison, school, rehabilitation centers and more. Overall, Mindfulness has stand out as a complete and independent support system for treating psychological disorders as well as for betterment of persona on multiple aspects.

Chapter 5: What is Mindfulness, and Why Should I Care?

In the Oxford English Dictionary, mindfulness is described as: "A mental state achieved by focusing one's awareness on the present moment, while calmly acknowledging and accepting one's feelings, thoughts, and bodily sensations, used as a therapeutic technique" (N.d.); and Davis and Hayes define mindfulness as "a moment-to-moment awareness of one's experience without judgment" (2012). Mindfulness isn't a long, time-consuming, endeavor that requires substantial classes or a doctorate degree to practice. Mostly, it simply necessitates a basic knowledge and a little bit of discipline in order to find which techniques work best for you in your life, when you can fit them in, and the determination to follow through.

As we are discussing mindfulness, it is important to take time to note that, because they are used interchangeably, mindfulness can easily be mistaken for meditation; but in reality, they are two different things. Mindfulness is the practice of being aware in the moment and understanding what is happening in your environment, thoughts, feelings, and emotions. Meditation is better understood as being aware internally and it is defined by the Oxford English Dictionary as "thinking deeply or focusing one's mind for a period of time, in silence or with the aid of chanting, for religious or spiritual purposes or as a method of relaxation" (N.d.). While meditation is often used as a piece of the mindfulness puzzle, it is not able to complete the entire picture.

It is often thought that mindfulness has its roots solidly in Buddhism; however, Trousselard et al. reminds us that "It is important to include that some commentators argue that the history of mindfulness should not be reduced to Buddhism and Hinduism, as mindfulness also has roots in Judaism, Christianity, and Islam (2014). Meditation and mindfulness aren't new concepts to humanity, and they both have been practiced for centuries upon centuries throughout different portions of the world, from Asia and the Middle East all the way to Native Americans. Because of its religious and philosophical ties, some people tend to have reservations about practicing mindfulness; however, following copious amounts of scientific research on the physical, emotional, and social benefits, mindfulness has itself been expanded upon and transformed into a secular way of connecting with oneself, nature, and others without said ties. It can be easily practiced in a secular or non-secular manner, depending on your preference.

Research on the benefits of mindfulness started gaining strong traction around 1979 with a man named Jon Kabat-Zinn, who is considered one of the pioneers of mindfulness practice. Jon Kabat Zinn has researched and taught at the University of Massachusetts for several decades and continues to work there to date of this publishing. He founded the Center for Mindfulness in Medicine, Health Care, and Society. His profile on the Center for Mindfulness website states that "his major research interests have focused on mind/body interactions for healing, clinical applications of mindfulness meditation training, the effects of MBSR [Mindfulness Based Stress Reduction] on the brain, on the immune system, and on healthy emotional expression while under stress; on healing (skin clearing rates) in people with psoriasis; on patients undergoing bone marrow transplantation; with prison inmates and staff; in multicultural settings;

and on stress in various corporate settings and work environments" (N.d.). Jon Kabat-Zinn has produced numerous books on the subject of mindfulness, and several of them will be in the "Additional Mindfulness Resources" section at the end of this book.

After Kabat-Zinn's introduction of mindfulness into the secular world, it has become a popular way to promote healing in the mind, body, and soul. The research has extended exponentially beyond what it originated as, both as religious practices and what Jon Kabat Zinn brought to the world. Below we will discuss the value of mindfulness and the science behind it.

Value of Mindfulness

While it is important to understand the origin of any practice, it is equally or potentially even more important to understand the empirical research and results before making any decisions about adaptation; and with mindfulness, the research is present! The research has proven that mindfulness can be beneficial in many areas of life, and because of this, no matter where you are in your journey, you can always reap the rewards of practicing mindfulness. According to the Mindfulness in Schools Project "amongst adults there is reasonably strong evidence for the positive impact of mindfulness on a wide range of mental and physical health conditions, on social and emotional skills and wellbeing, and on learning and cognition" (Weare, 2012); therefore, because of the far-reaching benefits of mindfulness, anyone can improve their well-being by utilizing the techniques. Weare goes on to claim that "there is also good evidence from neuroscience and brain imaging that mindfulness meditation reliably and profoundly alters the structure and function of the brain to improve the quality of both thought and feeling." Mindfulness is an incredible tool that does not require a significant amount of training on the basic level. With a small amount of discipline and the right techniques, everyone can benefit from this practice!

Jon Kabat-Zinn and his fellow researchers at the Center for Mindfulness in Medicine,

Health Care, and Society state about their research that "our work over the past thirty-five years has shown consistent, reliable, and reproducible demonstrations of major and clinically relevant reductions in medical and psychological symptoms across a wide range of medical diagnoses, including many different chronic pain conditions, other medical diagnoses and in medical patients with a secondary diagnosis of anxiety and/or panic, over the eight weeks of the MBSR intervention, and maintenance of these changes in some cases for up to four years of follow-up" (N.d., Center for Mindfulness). Not only will mindfulness be beneficial to mental health, but it can also effectively help those who live in chronic pain and/or a disability. Kabat-Zinn et al. continue the thought by claiming that "we have also seen consistent, reliable, and reproducible demonstrations of significant and clinically relevant increases in trait measures which are usually stable in adulthood, indicative of enhanced psychological hardiness (Kobasa) and greater sense of coherence (Antonovsky) over the course of the eight week intervention, and maintenance of these gains for up to three years of follow-up. The latter measures indicate a heightened sense of self and self-in-relationship, and a greater ability to find coherence and act effectively under high degrees of stress. These changes enhance the experience of self-efficacy in patients and their view of the value of engaging in their own on-going health and well-being through meditation, yoga, and above all, the systematic cultivation of awareness [Kabat-Zinn, Skillings, and Salmon, manuscript submitted]" (N.d., Center for Mindfulness).

Reaching further into the benefits of mindfulness, David & Hayes are even more deeply specific in what mindfulness can accomplish for you. These benefits include:

Decreased stress: there are copious amounts of research surrounding how mindfulness can help limit stress, in fact, "researchers concluded that mindfulness-based therapy may be useful in altering affective and cognitive processes that underlie multiple clinical issues" (David & Hayes, 2012). Therefore, mindfulness not only reduces stress, but it also rewires our brains in a way that changes how we handle stress! Furthermore, "researchers found that the participants who experienced mindfulness-based stress reduction had significantly less anxiety, depression and somatic distress compared with the control group. These findings suggest that mindfulness meditation shifts people's ability to use emotion regulation strategies in a way that enables them to experience emotion selectively, and that the emotions they experience may be processed differently in the brain…" (David & Hayes, 2012).

Decreased rumination: have you ever repeatedly ran something through your head? Thinking about it over, and over, and over; usually to your detriment? Then you'll be happy to know that "several studies have shown that mindfulness reduces rumination. In one study, for example, Chambers et al. (2008) asked 20 novice meditators to participate in a 10-day intensive mindfulness meditation retreat. After the retreat, the meditation group had significantly higher self-reported mindfulness and a decreased negative affect compared with a control group. They also experienced fewer depressive symptoms and less rumination" (David & Hayes, 2012).

Increased flexible cognition: according to David & Hayes, there was a research study which "found that people who practice mindfulness meditation appear to develop the skill of self-observation" (2012); this practice can help us understand not only ourselves but also our reactions to others, our environment, and our own emotions.

Positive Relationships: when looking at relationships, David & Hayes share that "the ability to respond well to relationship stress and the skill in communicating one's emotions to a partner. Empirical evidence suggests that mindfulness protects against the emotionally stressful effects of relationship conflict (Barnes et al., 2007), is positively associated with the ability to express oneself in various social situations

(Dekeyser el al., 2008) and predicts relationship satisfaction (Barnes et al., 2007; Wachs & Cordova, 2007)" (2012). The more we are able to slow down, be present in the moment, and notice what is happening around us, the more improved we will be with interacting with our friends, co-workers, significant others, and any additional people in our space. Surely when asking most people what comes to mind when they think of the concept of mindfulness, better relationships is not necessarily what comes to mind right away.

While the above benefits alone are enough to practice mindfulness, science tells us there are many more. Copious amounts of research have been completed around the world, and here are only a few of the additional benefits the researchers have found over the last several decades.

Managing anger: Meditation, which is a part of mindfulness, has been shown through a study (completed by DeSteno, Lim, Duong, & Condon) to discourage a response of aggression when provoked. This is completed through building awareness of emotion and how to successfully work through them. In other words, practicing mindfulness can be used as an anger management tool; although it is important to note that mindfulness in and of itself is not a replacement for anger management therapy if it is needed. It is simply a tool to use in the building of a better life.

Increase Focus: Zeidan et al. studied the effects of brief mindfulness training and found the incredible discovery that "after four sessions of either meditation training or listening to a recorded book, participants with no prior meditation experience were assessed with measures of mood, verbal fluency, visual coding, and working memory. Both interventions were effective at improving mood, but only brief meditation training reduced fatigue, anxiety, and increased mindfulness. Moreover, brief mindfulness training significantly improved visuospatial processing, working memory, and executive functioning" (2010). This research is proof that significant training in mindfulness is not needed in order to gain the benefits from the practice of it.

Decrease pain in chronic patients: When doing research on the effectiveness of mindfulness in the reduction of pain in chronic patients, Reiner, Tibi, & Lipsitz shore that out of the sixteen studies that they reviewed, they found the "in most studies (10 of 16), there was significantly decreased pain intensity in the MBI [Mindfulness Based Intervention] group. Findings were more consistently positive for samples limited to clinical pain (9 of 11). In addition, most controlled trials (6 of 8) reveal higher reductions in pain intensity for MBIs compared with control groups. Results from follow-up assessments reveal that reductions in pain intensity were generally well maintained" (2013); the key here is that not only did mindfulness-based interventions significantly reduce the intensity of the pain, but that it also worked for on-going maintenance and pain control.

Decrease in sleep issues: Anderson et al. found mindfulness to be significantly helpful in the reduction of sleep loss and in the increased ability for sleep. They share that "MBSR had a statistically significant effect on sleep quality just after the intervention but no long-term effect among breast cancer patients" (2013); therefore, it is important to note that if mindfulness is being used to improve sleep that it will need to be used on an on-going basis in order to continue to reap the benefits of the practice on sleep quality.

Chapter 6: How to be Mindful

You've learned what mindfulness is from the previous chapter and some reasons on why you should be practicing it. Now that you have an idea on what it is about and its importance, it is the right time to know how you would be able to practice it. What are the things you can do or the things you can follow in order to start being mindful of the things around you? How can you start being mindful by incorporating it into your daily life? Well, here are some steps you can try in order to jump start your mindfulness training.

One thing at a time

You are not supposed to multitask things because when in order to become mindful, you have to put your heart and soul in everything you do. You should be aiming for the best, for somethings that will make you stand out from the rest and paying only half of your attention to the work at hand will only lessen the quality of your work. So do one thing at a time and give all your focus and attention to the job at hand. Do your best in each of the tasks you do so you would not have to repeat it over again.

Do not rush

Never ever try and rush your way into doing the things that you must do because it just leads to being less productive. Also, being mindful means that you think about what you are doing so make deliberate actions that are precise and accurate so that you do not waste a second of your time instead of rushing things head-on and ending up wasting more time.

Stop worrying

Admit it; everyone has been worried at some point of their lives. It may be for a thousand of different reasons like when you think about the probability of your boss giving you that raise in salary or if you will pass that entrance exam for the college you've applied in. At a point, you were subjected to think, doubt and rethink again on what you can do to make things better. But the big question is: Were you even a bit happy during those anxious times? The answer is a big no. And that is the first big change you should make in order to be a happier person. Just let all the worries go. It may seem hard at first; you need to believe that eventually, everything will fall into place. Try to live a life that is stress-free. In order to do this, you need to find things that make you happy, things that you are very passionate about. Do that now. Remove your worries and just go with the flow of life. Do not worry about things that have not happened yet and focus on the now instead. Release your mind and your soul and just have fun with your life.

Be present in conversations

When you are talking to someone, it is very important to be mindful of them, especially of what they are thinking and what they are feeling. You need to focus on them in order to identify these things properly and interpret them the right way. This is why you must take part in conversations and actually be present in them. You need to not just make it seem that you are interested and that you care but actually be interested and actually care. You have to pick the right words to say and you can only do that by actually listening to what the person talking to you is saying. So you better pay attention.

Savour food

Mindfulness can also be practiced by what is called mindful eating. It is mainly composed of savoring your food. Do not rush on eating, try to taste the different flavor your dishes might offer your taste buds. Let them take you to places you have never been to just yet. Enjoy the meal you eat every single time. This way, you will get to remember what each dish taste like and get to be surprised by what you find new every time you get to eat again.

Live in the moment

It may be hard to do but you have to learn to live in the moment. Let the past take care of itself and forget about the things that are yet to happen. Just take the present for what it is and actually have fun living in it. Do the things you want to do today regardless of how it is related to your past or future. Just keep on going and doing the things that you like and go for what your passion is. Sometimes, what you do now would not matter that much in the future. After all, the future holds a lot of secrets that are not known to you, and you do not know how long you have to live in this world so you might as well get to enjoy it as much as you can.

Accept your weak points

In order to be more mindful of other people, it would be good to know what your weak points are and actually accept them. You just have to remember that nobody is perfect and there is no reason for you to be insecure of them. You need to embrace them and keep in mind that these imperfections are what make you the person you are right now. It does not matter if you have many weak points because once you have learned to accept them, you would know how to manage them or even get over them. Knowing your weak points can be turned into your strength if you know how to use them right.

Try meditating through cooking and cleaning

There are a lot of mundane tasks that you do every day on a repetitive basis, and you would have an idea on what they are by now. Think about using these tasks to maximize your way into being mindful. What you can do is this: meditate while you are doing these tasks so that you get to save time and have a dual purpose for the tasks. For example, you can try it while you are cooking for breakfast, dinner or lunch or maybe when you are cleaning your room or cleaning your house. It saves you the effort of finding the time you need to meditate and it is certainly just like hitting two birds with one stone.

Walking meditation

When you think of meditation you mostly think that you are just going to sit there and take deep breaths with your eyes closed. Well, that is just the traditional way of meditating. In the modern days, there are meditations that can be done in your everyday life. For example, walking meditation is done by focusing your steps on the earth, the land you are stepping on, letting go of all your thoughts. You just bring your attention to each step you take until you finally reach your destination.

Keep a journal

Another way to be mindful is to keep a journal, something to write all your thoughts about and all the things that have happened to you during the day. It may come in a form of a notebook or a laptop journal since most things are paperless nowadays. Just go and write or type away and you will notice that doing this helps you in noticing the small things that you did not notice right away and it also helps in gathering your thoughts. Another thing about keeping a journal is that it makes every day a whole lot more personal than just letting another day pass by. It makes you more appreciative of the now.

Go for Yoga

Like meditation, practicing yoga can also be a great practice for turning to your inner self and slowing your fast paced life down. One of the most important elements in yoga is to focus your breath. This is because it brings a person's attention to what is currently happening as of the very moment and it certainly brings away all the other distractions in your life. You can go and try a new yoga post each day so that you would not get bored of it and also because different yoga positions have different functions for your body. It will also challenge you and practice to be mindful is a whole lot easier while doing yoga because you are clear of the most common distractions that you have during your daily activities. Thus, including yoga in your daily routine is a great idea.

Putting space in between

Try not to schedule your tasks to close and leave some time in between your work. This way, it would be easier to adjust if some emergency happens or you get too tired from work. It can be a time for resting before your next schedule but it is also a way of preparing for the next task at hand. It also relieves stress for you because you would not have to rush to the next schedule. So do not work yourself too hard and try putting some spaces in between your schedule.

Do less

The problem with tasks is that when you pile them up, they end up being a mess that you have a harder problem to deal with. So do less so that you are able to finish them all in a proper way. Stop being in a rush, let things fall in the right way. In reality, this is just a matter of prioritizing and deciding which tasks are really urgent and important and which are the ones you can still do later on if you have the time.

5 minutes a day

Take at least 5 minutes off each day and just rest during that time. You can also do this so you can exercise focusing on things. For example, focus on the way your watch ticks and just stare at it for 5 minutes. Or just sit back, relax and close your tired eyes for a bit. Just do something that would not stress you. It may not look much but in the long run, these 5 minutes a day will eventually pay off. After all, the small things will eventually pile up into bigger and better things if you keep on doing them.

Making Rituals out of chores

It has been discussed previously that you can actually meditate while doing your daily chores, well, aside from that, you can actually make your daily chores into what is known as rituals. For example, while you are cleaning your yard, you most probably think about just doing it later or that it sucks to be doing it. Instead of thinking that way, you should treat it more importantly as if not cleaning your yard would make your day incomplete. Do this with every mundane chore that you have and things would be set out for the better.

Take in the beauty of your surroundings

Most days, you just rush your way to work or to school or to wherever you are bound to go. You do not take the time to notice the beauty of the place that you are passing through. You do not even take a second to look at the things around you. This is where mindfulness comes in. when you try to take in the beauty of the little details around you, you become more mindful so take a few minutes of your time and appreciate it.

These are just some of the steps that you can take in order to be a whole lot more mindful than your current state. By doing them, you are set to a more mindful life and you can say that you truly are living for bigger things in life and the present. The next chapter will discuss some daily activities that you can apply in your everyday life; simple things that you can fit in your busy schedule.

Chapter 7: Mindfulness Exercises that Involve the Body

As they say, the body is the temple of the soul. Most of the time, you may find that the physical pain that you deal with every day may not even be caused by your movement but the stress that your mind is experiencing constantly.

In addition, being mindful of how your body reacts to your environment would allow you to find areas in your body that would react positively or negatively to the energies that are around you. For that reason, there are mindfulness exercises that helps relax the body to relieve stress and help you become aware of sensations that you regularly feel.

Whenever you are feeling that your body is in pain, or that your stress is so overwhelming that it begins to affect your body, here are some of the mindfulness techniques that you can practice.

1. Deep breathing

To practice deep breathing techniques for relaxation, it would be advisable to choose a great location that would allow you to assume different poses. Great choices would be a park or a garden. However, you can do this technique in your own living room.

The key to properly do this technique is to breathe deeply from the abdomen and get as much air as you can into your lungs. The more oxygen you let inside your lungs, the less anxious and short of breath you feel. Here is how you can do it:

Sit comfortably on a mat and assume that position with a straight back. Put a hand on your chest, and the other one over your stomach. If you are having difficulty breathing while sitting up, lie down on the mat instead. You can place a book or any light but flat object over your stomach if you are lying down.

Close your eyes and then breathe deeply through your nose. You know that you are breathing properly if the hand over your stomach rises and the other hand on your chest moves very little.

Now, exhale slowly through your mouth. Push out as much air as you can as you contract your abdominal muscles. Count from one to ten in your head as you exhale.

6. Body Scan Meditation

This technique works by becoming aware of the different sensations that occur in different parts of your body. Here is how you can do it:

On a mat, lie on your back with your legs uncrossed. Relax your arm on your sides. You can choose to open or close your eyes.

Breathe deeply and focus on your breaths. Your abdomen should rise and fall as you breathe. Do this for two minutes.

Shift your focus on the toes on your right foot. Pay attention to the sensations that you feel on that area. Now, focus on those sensations as you pay attention to your breathing. Do the same to the sole of your foot. Imagine that the air you breathe in flows down to that area. Do that for two minutes.

Shift the focus to the rest of your legs, including both your right and your left side alternatively, and tune in to the sensations starting from your calf all the way up to your thighs.

From there, shift your attention to your torso and pay attention to the sensations you feel in your lower back and abdomen. If you feel certain areas in that region that is experiencing pain or any type of discomfort, pay attention to them, and mentally will them to relax.

Shift the attention to your fingers, then to your elbows and your arms. Afterwards, move towards your shoulders, neck, and head. Put more focus on your head, and focus on your temples.

Once you reach the top of your head, imagine that you are looking at yourself from above. Lay still and focus on your breathing. Note how your body is, and how much you feel relaxed. Afterwards, do some stretching.

7. Muscle Tension Release

This mindfulness exercise involves paying attention to your tense muscles and releasing the stress from your aching muscles suddenly. You can do this exercise while standing, sitting, or lying, depending on what position you are most comfortable with. Here's how you can do it:

Close your eyes. Let your mind focus on the tension in your hands. Try to pay attention on the tiredness that you feel on your palms and on your wrists.

Clench your fists tightly and take deep breathes. Afterwards, abruptly unclench your fists, releasing the tension quickly.

Tighten your stomach muscles and hold in your breath. Release the tightness quickly, like you did with your fists.

Focus on your head by furrowing your eyebrows and closing your eyes tightly. Tighten the muscles on your lips as well. Release the tenseness abruptly.

Continue to do this throughout each muscle group in your body.

Take deep breaths, and stretch.

Chapter 8: Starting On Your Own

One if the core principle of meditation is concentration. You need to repeat a phrase, word or mantra, or focus on your breathing while allowing your thoughts to come and go. Concentration meditation exercises such as that of mindful exercises, tai chi and yoga will induce in you a relaxation response. This relaxation response will allow your body to reduce response to stress.

Mindfulness builds upon these concentration practices. Here is how mindfulness exercises work.

Enables you to go with the flow. Mindfulness exercises allows you to establish and build up concentration. You are able to notice and focus on the flow of your innermost emotions, thoughts and bodily sensations without judging them.

Enables you to pay attention to the world around you. Mindfulness exercises allows you to observe the external sensations around you such as sights, touch and sounds. You are able to live in the present and experience life more. The principle of mindfulness is on to fixate on a singular idea, sensation or emotion or get caught up thinking of the past or the future, rather you are supposed to sense what comes and leaves your, and to realize the mental habits that gives you the feeling of well-being and the mental habits that produce suffering.

You keep on practices. For some people, the processes of mindfulness may it be relaxing, but you should remember that it helps you find greater joy and keeps you self-aware. As time goes on, you will learn to be more comfortable with a wide range of experiences.

Practicing Acceptance

Another of the core principles of mindfulness is the acceptance of awareness. You need to accept any feeling that arises in your awareness at every moment. You need to be kind and forgiving to yourself.

Mindfulness involves redirecting your mind when it strays off. During your mindfulness exercises, it is likely that you may start to daydream, plan or think about the past. When this happens you need to gently redirect your mind back to the sensations present.

Keep on practicing. The best way to take advantage of mindfulness is to keep on practices. You should dedicate time to mindfulness exercises and if you miss those sessions you should start again.

Learn to accept the experiences you have during meditation and mindfulness exercises. You need to learn to accept the sensations at hand during meditation. As you practice mindfulness exercises you also learn to accept the things that you feel for the rest of the day.

Make Mindfulness A Daily Activity

It is a good idea to make mindfulness exercises a daily activity in addition to the dedicated sessions you have in the week. You should practice mindfulness by focusing on moment-to-moment sensations as you go about your day. You can give your undivided attention to singular tasks such as flossing your teeth or petting your dog or even eating a meal.

You should focus on the present as you perform these activities.

Simple exercises you can try out right now

Here are two exercises you can try out right now and on your own.

Practicing Mindfulness Meditation

Simple Exercise 1

present?
present?
present?
present?

This exercise involves basic mindfulness meditations

Sit cross legged on a mat or on the floor. You can also sit on a straight-backed chair.

Focus on your breathing just a single aspect of it, such as the feeling of the air flowing into your nostrils and out again. You can also focus on the rising and falling of your belly as you inhale and exhale. Focus on this in and out sensation unlike your full concentration is on it.

Now begin to widen your focus outwards and inwards. Focus on the sensations on your skin, the sounds around you that you are failing to hear and the thoughts and ideas that flows through your mind.

You should accept and embrace these ideas, thoughts and sensations without any judgements at all. If you feel your mind racing or wandering off, you need to refocus it to your breathing and then begin again.

Simple Exercise 2

The next exercise is another simple one and is also a less formal approach to mindfulness. This should be practice on a daily basis. It should help keep you focus on the right now. You should pick a singular task within with you can perform that task while performing the mindfulness exercise. The task can be shaving, or showering or taking a walk or playing with your dog.

You should focus your attention to the sensations of your body.

Now you should start breathing through your nose, while noticing the air flowing downwards into your lower belly. Bring your attention to your abdomen expanding fully.

Then exhale through your mouth.

Focus on the sensations of repeated inhalation and exhalation.

Now proceed to doing the task you have picked to perform. You should perform this task with deliberation and intent. Engaging all your senses. Notice the touch of your fingers, the sight and the sounds produces. Savor the sensations fully.

If you notice tour mind wandering off, you should bring your mind back to the task and sensation at hand.

Invest You Time

Mindfulness like any other beneficial activity, you benefit when you invest in yourself. Jon Kabat-Zinn, renowned in the field of mindfulness recommends that you practice mindfulness exercises about 45 minutes a day, six times a week. However, you can start slowly. You can practice the exercises described above for short periods of time every day.

As you have noticed it does not take much to get started. I assume that since you are reading this book, you are committed to being mindful.

Chapter 9: Deep Breathing For Stress Relief

There is no simpler way to practice mindfulness breathing other than by simply focusing your attention on your breath as you inhale and exhale. To do this, you can assume any comfortable sitting or lying position with your eyes either closed or open. It is best to close your eyes to keep off visual distractions.

Setting out a designated time for this mindful exercise helps you make it a daily habit, but you can also practice it whenever you feel stressed or anxious.

When trying to calm your nerves in very stressful situations, it might be helpful if you start by taking in some exaggerated breath: a deep inhalation through your nose that can last only about 3 seconds, hold your breath for another 2 seconds, and then a long exhalation through your mouth that can last about 4 seconds.

Focusing on the rise and fall of your chest as you breathe or the sensation of the breath rushing through your nostrils helps you maintain awareness.

Steps to a Stress-Relieving Mindful Breathing Exercise

Find one relaxed, comfortable position—whether in your home, school, or office. You can sit on the floor, cushion, or chair. Keep your back upright but do not let it be too tight or tense and keep your hands rested wherever they feel comfortable on your body. You can place your tongue on the roof of your mouth if you are comfortable with that.

Notice and keep your body relaxed. Try noticing things like the shape of your body and your body weight. Relax and be curious about your body: the sensations, the connection with the surface you sit on, the touch, etc. Relax any part where you notice tension or tightness and just breathe.

Tune fully into your breath and feel the natural flow of breath-in and out of your airways. You do not have to do anything to your breath; do not shorten or lengthen it, just watch the natural inflow and outflow of breaths. Notice where you feel the breath in the body—perhaps you feel it most in your abdomen, chest, throat, or nostrils. See if it is possible to feel the sensation of your breath one at a time. Know when one breath ends and when another begins.

Your mind may start wandering as you do this. You may find yourself thinking about other things. This occurrence is not a problem. In fact, such is very natural. Just take note of the fact that your mind is wandering and gently redirect your attention back to your breaths.

You can stay here for about 5-7 minutes. Notice your breath in silence. You will lose yourself in thought from time to time, but always bring yourself back to your breaths.

After a couple of minutes, once again take note of your body, your entire body seated here. Allow yourself to fall into deeper relaxation and reward yourself for practicing for the day.

Let us now look at how you can use visualization and guided imagery to deal with stress.

Visualization And Guided Imagery For Enhanced Stress Relief

Visualization and guided imagery offer you yet another avenue to become more mindful of yourself and in so doing, win the fight against stress. These mindful techniques involve the systematic practice of creating a detailed mental picture of a peaceful and attractive setting/environment.

Guided imagery acts as an element of distraction aimed at redirecting your attention away from whatever is stressing you and directing it towards a more calming focus. In essence, the guided imagery technique is a direct suggestion to your body and your unconscious mind to behave as though the peaceful, safe, and relaxing environment you have imagined is real and present.

Guided imagery relies on nothing more than your own imagination and ability to concentrate. This ability is always at your disposal provided you are not exhausted. However, like every other technique that requires mental concentration, this practice is most successful when you practice it in private settings where you are most likely to practice without any interruptions.

Steps to Guided Imagery

Here are steps you can take to enjoy the stress-relieving effects of guided imagery:

Find a very private calm place and make yourself as comfortable as possible.

Take a couple of deep slow breaths to center your attention.

Close your eyes.

Imagine yourself being in a beautiful location where everything is exactly the way you wish it should be such as a beach, forest, or mountain.

Once in that imaginary environment, imagine yourself becoming calm and relaxed. Alternatively, you can imagine yourself feeling, smiling, having a good time, or being plain happy.

Focus on the sensory attributes in your imagined environment to make it more vivid in your mind. For instance, if you imagine the beach, spend some time in vivid imagination of the sensation of the warm sun on your skin, the smell of the ocean, salt spray, seaweed, sound of the wave, seagulls and wind. The entire image becomes more vivid with more invocation of your senses.

Stay in your imagined scene and tour the whole of its sensory aspects for 5-10 minutes or until you feel completely relaxed.

While relaxed, tell yourself you can always return to that scene whenever you feel like relaxing.

Open your eyes and return to the real world around you.

It is important to point out that meditation techniques are not the only exercises you can engage in to help you relax and feel less stressed.

We also have a number of physical exercises you can incorporate into your daily life to help you keep winning against stress. When you add mindfulness to these exercises, their effects can be as mind-blowing as they are amazing.

Let us now look at mindful physical exercises as part of your daily stress-beating habits:

Mindful Physical Workouts For Stress Relief

You need physical exercises to enjoy optimum health and sustain your overall personal well-being.

Below are benefits of a physical workout regimen:

Pumps up your endorphins

According to various research studies, physical activities help increase the production of your brain's feel-good neurotransmitters called endorphins. You can induce increased endorphin production by engaging in something as simple as a rousing game of tennis or a hike down the village mountain. With this increased endorphin comes the high spirits you need to get out of the stress web.

Meditation in motion

Whenever you engage in a fast-paced game such as soccer or racquetball, if you are mindful enough, you will notice you have easily forgotten about all the issues of life that make you bitter, anxious, depressed, and stressed. This is because you have concentrated on nothing but the movement of your body during these physical exercises. In addition, the resulting energy and optimism from these workouts will help you stay calmer for longer with enhanced mental clarity to address issues as they arise.

Most forms of physical exercise can help you stay fit and reduce stress. However, it is always important that you do what you love and engage in exercises you derive pleasure from such as climbing the stairs to your office floor instead of the usual practice of using the elevator, yoga, bicycling, gardening, swimming, jogging, skiing, skating, weightlifting, gymnastics, etc.

Chapter 10: USING MINDFULNESS TO DEAL WITH ADDICTIONS

You can use mindfulness in addition to the techniques you are using to deal with addiction. Please note that you cannot rely on mindfulness alone to deal with addiction. You will definitely need the help of a psychologist or therapist. Thus, mindfulness is more like an add-on to dealing with addictions. Let us see how mindfulness can help you deal with your addictions.

Mindfulness For Coping With Addiction

It can be really tough for addicts who find themselves going back to the same habits after they had promised themselves never to indulge in it again.

Mindfulness can be a very useful technique to recover from addictions because it allows you to become more aware of things that you are trying to avoid and the reasons that you have for trying to avoid them. Mindfulness helps you deal with your cravings non-judgmentally and helps you to be kinder to yourself. When your emotions and desires are under control, you are more likely to make better choices.

Sometimes, just acknowledging and observing your cravings and allowing the craving to subside without doing anything about it enough to make your cravings go away. Therefore, the next time you are craving something you really don't want to abuse, you should do the following:

Find a comfortable sitting position and sit with your back straight.

Breathe in and out, slowly to allow your body to relax. Don't try to control your breath, just breathe.

Now, imagine that you can see your breath going in and out of your body.

Continue to breathe slowly and avoid having your mind wander. If it does wander, just slowly bring it back.

Do this each time the craving comes and keep at it until the craving passes. You will notice that gradually, you will be able to control your cravings and make healthier choices that would make you feel better.

Mindfulness For Smoking Cessation

It is no longer news that smoking is harmful to your health, even the manufacturers do not try to deny it. However, it is impossible to deny the fact that it is extremely difficult to stop the habit.

The good news is that simple mindfulness exercises like mindful smoking can help you cope with tobacco cravings so that you can eventually stop smoking. It is not going to make you stop in one day but gradually as you practice the exercise, your cravings will reduce, and you will be able to make smarter choices.

Start by looking at the pack of cigarettes you are about to smoke.

Read the warnings on the label.

Reflect deeply on the warnings and try to visualize some of the health implications.

Light it and feel the cigarette between your fingers.

Don't think about anything else or try to judge your feelings or actions, just smoke.

Taste and perceive the smell of the smoke in your mouth.

Think about the health implications and visualize them without judgments.

Continue to feel, smell, and observe the smoke until you finish the stick.

Mindful smoking helps you become aware of the implications of what you are doing. It helps you weigh the costs and benefits of smoking alongside each other so that you can make better choices in the future.

Smoking absentmindedly is how you continue to indulge yourself but when you engage in mindful smoking, you may be able to clearly see that it is not worth it and you can gradually reduce how many cigarettes you smoke in a day until you overcome the addiction.

MINDFULNESS TECHNIQUES FOR DEALING WITH OTHER PROBLEMS

In this last chapter, we will look at other problems that you can deal with using mindfulness techniques

Mindfulness For Eating Disorders And Weight Management

Mindfulness can also be beneficial for people suffering from eating disorders like compulsive overeating, anorexia, bulimia, and binge eating. People who suffer from these disorders usually suffer from negative thoughts and emotions concerning their body image so they end up developing these habits with the hope that it would help them alter their bodies but most of the time, they end up with worse health challenges.

This mindful eating exercise can help you control your eating disorders.

Shut out any distractions from your phone, the internet, TV or any other distractions when you are about to eat. Focus solely on the eating experience.

Take a deep breath.

For a few minutes, focus on how your body feels and try to see your body as a friend, a friend that needs to be nurtured and nourished.

Look at your food and think positively about it. Think of all the beautiful benefits your body will enjoy from eating this healthy meal.

Start eating mindfully, savor the tastes of each spoonful that goes into your mouth without judgment.

Imagine the food passing through your body, supplying energy and nutrients to all parts of your body that need nourishment.

Doing this each time you eat will help you develop a healthier relationship with food to help you deal with whatever eating disorder you are suffering from.

Mindfulness For Obsessive Compulsive Disorders (OCD}

If you suffer from obsessive compulsive disorder, you find it very difficult to live in, and enjoy the present moment. You are likely to be always worrying and obsessing about things in the past or the future, what is going wrong and all of that. The downside is that many times, these assessments are incorrect and happen because of something called Cognitive-distortion.

Cognitive distortion is a condition where you believe that when you think about doing bad things, it is almost the same as performing actions associated with the thoughts. Therefore, when you think about not shutting the door, it means you haven't shut it so you continue to shut the door each time you think of the door.

Relaxation techniques like mindfulness meditation can be very useful for OCD sufferers. You will find the breathing space meditation described in the previous chapter very effective if you are suffering from OCD. It sends a strong relaxation signal to the brain so that you can be calm and relaxed instead of obsessing about things.

Mindfulness For Insomnia

This research carried out at the Harvard Medical School revealed that mindfulness is very effective for fighting insomnia and inducing sleep. Drifting thoughts and failing to live in the moment is one of the major causes of insomnia. You can try out this exercise to help you sleep the next time you are lying in bed and unable to sleep.

Lie in your bed.

Direct your attention to your breathing.

Imagine that the air you are breathing is coming from a far distance; observe as it gets into your body and out as you exhale.

Try to observe the air; is it cool or warm? Is there any scent? Can you taste the air in your mouth?

Continue to breathe in and out and count each breath you exhale.

If your mind drifts, bring it back slowly and refocus.

Continue to do this until you sleep off. If you still can't sleep after doing this for about forty minutes, introduce the body scan relaxation while still lying in bed. This should help you sleep eventually.

Chapter 11: Mindfulness Meditation Step-by-Step

When you begin this type of meditation, you do need to be away from people and distractions. This helps you to get the hang of meditating but when you are more experienced, you can use mindfulness meditation in other areas of your life even when you are in the company of others. For the simplicity of the exercise, we need to create a certain ambiance. Thus being alone in a quiet place will help you to start this journey. You need to be dressed in comfortable clothing and to be seated in a position that respects your posture.

Step One – Seating position

The pose that you take depends upon your mobility. If you are able to sit on a cushion on a yoga mat, then you would be expected to bend your knees and cross your ankles. Your back should be straight at all times.

If you are unable to sit on the floor because of lack of mobility, that doesn't matter. Find a hard chair and sit with your feet flat on the floor and place your hands in your lap. If you have a chair that leans backward, try to sit with your back straight up because posture is very important.

You do not have to close your eyes although if you wish to, you can light a candle to give you something to focus on.

Step Two – Concentrate on your breathing and position

Be aware of your leg position and your arm position. Be aware of your seating position and don't stiffen your back. Yes, you need to have it straight, but not stiff. Be aware of how your body feels. Start to breathe in through the nostrils and feel the energy going down into your body. Your upper abdomen forms a kind of pivot motion when you get the breathing at the right kind of rhythm. Breathe in and out and get the rhythm to your breathing even and controlled. Feel your body relax. Feel your mind relax.

Step three – Listen to the silence

Silence may be broken from time to time by interference from outdoor noises, the song of a bird or anything that happens within the moment that you are meditating. Accept the silence and also acknowledge and accept the interruptions, letting them simply be acknowledged and then let go of.

Step Four – Relax your eyes

Lower your eyes a little so you don't have to stare. Let them simply be aware of the world around you without having to search anything out. Let them relax.

Step Five – Be kind to your wandering mind

Expect your mind to wander. There is no need to analyze what you are thinking.

Simply accept the thought that enters your head and then acknowledge it. Don't let it enter your mind to such a degree that it is able to touch your emotions. Observe it and then let it go without using any kind of judgment at all. No matter what the **thought** is or what made it arise, simply acknowledge and let go.

Step 6 – Using your breathing to help you concentrate

The central focus during mindfulness meditation is your breath. If you find that this distracts you rather than helping you concentrate on the flame of the candle and when thoughts come into your mind, go back to that candle flicker and rest your mind. It is better if you can get back to the breathing being your focus because this is something you always have with you all the time and you can use this for meditating when you are in other places and want to allow your mind the benefit of meditation.

When you are distracted, go through the process of:

Acknowledgment

Looking without judging

Letting go

Getting back to your focus on your breathing.

When should you meditate?

You can make this something to start your day and meditate before breakfast. Simply set your alarm a little earlier and meditate before the world has woken up and come to life. You should never meditate after eating as you may have to deal with digestive problems. Another time that is good for mindful meditation is at sunset or before your evening meal.

How long to meditate

It's a good idea to make meditation part of your daily routine. Don't expect to find miraculous results straight away. You need time to get your mind accustomed to this way of behaving but the more you do it on a regular basis, the better you will become at it. I would suggest 20 minutes is quite sufficient for beginners and that more experienced meditators can choose their own amount of time.

At the end of meditation

Remember that your body and mind have slowed down. Your blood pressure will be lower and your heartbeat slower. Thus, when you finish meditation for the day, be slow to get back to your normal speed of living. I would use this time to write in a journal the things you can do in your next meditation practice to make your meditation better. This gives you time to transition back into your everyday life.

Chapter 12: What is Mindfulness?

Mindfulness is simply the art of paying more attention to details as they happen, becoming more aware of your immediate scenarios, environment and situations.

This is how Wikipedia puts it: "Mindfulness is a mental practice where a person becomes intentionally, but non-judgmentally aware of his/her thoughts and actions as they occur. Mindfulness can apply to bodily actions, the thoughts of the mind, and your feelings. It is possible for you to live a more mindful life and enjoy all the benefits of mindfulness. "

What it Means to Live a Mindful Life

Living a mindful life entails applying mindfulness to whatever you do wherever you do it, however you do it, and whenever you do it. For instance, when you are deeply engaged in your yoga practices, it takes mindfulness to get all the mental and physical benefits of that great exercise.

When you are engaged in mindful meditation, what makes your meditation sessions worth the effort and time you put into them is your level of mindfulness.

You can brush your teeth mindfully every morning by concentrating on the actions and the feelings they bring while you are it.

You can have mindful baths by savoring the sensation and feelings you experience when the warm water trickles down your back.

You can engage in mindful walking by feeling every step and noting how your body reacts as your feet touch the grass, earth, concrete, or whatever you are walking on.

You can engage in mindful dancing by feeling your body move and your taut muscles relax with each dance move and step

You can engage in mindful jogging, running, or any other physical exercises in the woods and enjoy the best of nature such as the beautiful and aerial sights and sounds or early morning blossoming flowers and chipping birds.

You can do your laundry mindfully and by so doing, feel more appreciative, and practice gratitude as you meditate on the fact that you have clothes to wear while many cannot wear their clothes because of one problem or are willing to wear but cannot do so because they do not have clothes to wear.

You can engage in mindful eating by relishing each bite and being more thankful of having food on the table and enjoying good nutrition options that help you stay healthy.

You can do anything with mindfulness and apply the mindfulness habit to all aspects of your life, and thereby harness the rich benefits of living a mindful life.

Let's see some major benefits of living a mindful life:

Benefits of Mindfulness

When mindfulness becomes a part of your life, you can be sure to experience positive changes in every aspect of your life.

Here are some of the major benefits of mindfulness:

Living more in the present

A mindful life will help you focus on what is happening around you and concentrate on tasks at hand with minimum distractions from past regrets, future worries, and uncertainties.

When you become mindful, you will understand why every second counts and make sure you do not allow the past get in the way of your ability to enjoy everything you should enjoy in the present.

Happy marriage and relationships

Most times, what strains marriages and relationships is lack or inadequacy of understanding. With mindfulness, you will understand your partner more, appreciate the efforts he or she makes to make things work in the marriage or relationship, and pay more attention to things your partner likes and do those things that keep them happy and committed to you.

Improved communication

When you are a more mindful person, you get more from interactions with people. When you mindfully engage people in conversations, mindfulness will help you pick up nonverbal cues and become better at emotional intelligence. This will help you read in-between what someone is saying and understand the hidden emotions and meanings in every word someone speaks.

Increased productivity

You cannot be a mindful person and not become more productive in your work life. Mindfulness helps you manage your time better, pay attention to tasks that are important and urgent over others, concentrate on one task at a time to get the best results, and do things with a touch of perfection.

A healthier mind

A mindful person gets to enjoy a more robust mental health. Most mental health problems like stress, anxiety, worry, fear and depression can easily be treated with practicing mindfulness. This will naturally lead to the development of a healthier mind.

Increased self-discipline

Becoming mindful and making mindfulness a part of your life will require daily mindful activities and practices. Most of these activities need consistent input until they become daily habits. It takes self-discipline to keep practicing even when you do not feel like it until you can effortlessly do things mindfully.

Higher self-esteem

Experts recommend mindful practices like mindful meditation as one of the techniques for fighting low self-esteem. Mindful practices such as visualization, positive affirmations, imagery, etc. help you develop greater self-respect and self-esteem.

Helps you manage stress

Mindfulness is an effective way to deal with high stress levels. With increased mindfulness in your life, and the more you engaged in mindful activities, the more you will experience enough calm and peace within and without to help you change the things you can change and accept what you cannot change in your life.

Better health

Mindfulness brings happiness and less worries. The fewer the issues you allow to get you worked up or increase your stress levels, the happier your life becomes and your health will automatically get a new breath of life.

To get the best from your mindful efforts, it is important that you give every area of your life attention by engaging in mindful practices and exercises that will help you get the best from mindful living.

Chapter 13: The Greatest Partner We All Have

The enigma of the mind has long intrigued us. Though we use our minds to think, question, and explore, what our minds are has been a mystery to us, which has been philosophically debated for centuries now.

Is the mind the brain? Or does the mind reside within the brain? Is it the soul? Can it exist outside of the human body? These are all questions that have been asked and deliberated over for years. Science, religion, and philosophy have all attempted to answer this question for us.

Yet despite the centuries we've spent pondering these questions, the mind still remains a mystery to us.

With the advent of modern science, scientists and doctors have turned to research our brains to find the answer to this question. Yet, what we know about the brain is only the tip of the iceberg.

We discuss our minds today because our mind also controls our mindfulness and consciousness.

However, before we can delve into mindfulness and consciousness, it is important to understand what these words really mean.

We have often heard the words consciousness and mindfulness thrown about in our daily lives. We tell little children to be mindful of their actions often. Yet, what do these words mean?

Consciousness is defined as the state of being aware of and responsive to one's surroundings. Consciousness is essentially awareness. Every moment we spent awake, we are in consciousness.

Mindfulness is the next step in consciousness. According to researchers, mindfulness is a psychological process of bringing one's attention to experience the present moment.

We have all experienced those moments in which our minds wander during a boring lecture in class or while at work. Those are moments when we are in consciousness, however not in mindfulness. Though we are awake and aware of our surroundings, we often take our surroundings and experiences for granted. We see life through a tinted glass, walking through our familiar life which we are no longer excited or surprised by. That is until something forces us to refocus our attention, at which point, we can now begin to be mindful.

Yet how do we attain this mindfulness? How can we connect consciousness and mindfulness at a glance? For this, we turn to meditation and other training of the mind which focuses on the present.

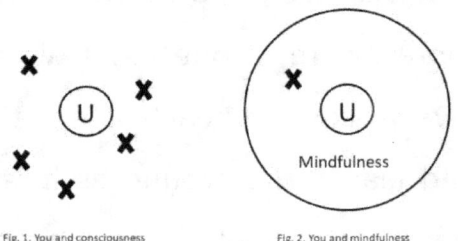

Fig. 1. You and consciousness   Fig. 2. You and mindfulness

Figure 1: The small circle in the figure represents you. The X's represent things around you, such as a sound of a car honking, the phone buzzing in our jacket pocket, or perhaps another person bumping into you as they rush past you. While in consciousness, we are aware of all these situations. We are in automatic mode going through our daily lives, reacting to any responses that come to us.

Figure 2: When we are practicing mindfulness, we draw a bigger circle around ourselves. We pay attention to and become more aware of one X. As we are walking, we focus on each step that touches and leaves the ground as it is in the moment. We can feel the hairs on our arms stand up as the breeze cools us down. We can feel our lungs inflate and deflate with every inhale and exhale. We microfocus on one of these and let our minds be full of this one single activity.

A simple way to understand mindfulness is to dissect the word itself - "mind" and "fullness." Your mind, as on the picture, is now full as you're now aware of your consciousness.

There are many challenges that we face in the context of mindfulness, as it is not an easy feat to achieve, especially in the modern world we live in, with a multitude of distractions.

When we are not mindful of our thinking, our minds will drift away, full of arbitrary thoughts.

Long ago, when man first roamed the earth as hunter-gatherers, our ancestors had a shorter to-do list. They simply had to go out hunt animals or gather berries, all the while looking out for predators and poisonous berries. They didn't have the complicated calendars filled with appointments, emails, phone calls, meetings, and deadlines that we do today.

Today, we are on information overload. We constantly throw so much information in our minds that it simply doesn't know how to process the enormous amount of data coming at it.

Think of our mind as a computer. Every computer has a certain limit on how much data it can handle, considering its RAM and processing speed. As the computer reaches its limit, it starts slowing down, eventually shutting down. We've all experienced opening far too many applications on our phones or computers only for it to shut down or freeze on us.

Similar to this, our minds will allocate a certain amount of energy to each of our tasks, such as a business proposal we need to put together or organize a birthday party for a friend.

When our minds are not able to accommodate all the tasks we must tend to, the feeling of stress and exhaustion sets in. We stop staying in the moment as our overloaded minds attempt to analyze and device an action plan. Like a computer, our minds start freezing up or slowing down.

Yet the moment we become aware of our thoughts, we can enter a state of mindfulness. We stop trying to analyze and device action plans and simply start noticing and becoming aware.

In a state of mindfulness, like a parade commander, we begin to take charge and give clear instructions to our mind, "we are going to do this first, take on the ground!" When we continue in this state of mindfulness for a prolonged period, we can then start to feel peaceful, in charge, and fully focused at the moment.

Since the late 1970's, research has been conducted on the stress-alleviating capabilities of mindfulness, with positive results, with many experts endorsing mindfulness for stress reduction.

Mindfulness meditation and practice have been adopted as a strategy by many health-care professionals. In fact, mindfulness is a crucial aspect of many forms of therapy that aim to treat depression, anxiety, and stress.

Mindfulness-based stress reduction (MBSR) utilizes meditation, body awareness, and yoga to help people become more mindful. Mindfulness-based cognitive therapy (MBCT) has quickly become one of the newer techniques used by professionals to treat chronic depression. Mindfulness is also a core part of dialectical behavior therapy (DBT), mode deactivation therapy (MDT), and acceptance and commitment therapy (ACT). [1]

However, mindfulness should not be viewed as just a reactionary therapy to treat mental-health issues once they have manifested themselves within us. Instead, we should also view it as a preventive strategy to stop the rise of mental health issues, as it helps people reduce worry and stress by focusing on the present, rather than the future or the past.

We can all practice mindfulness meditation, which involves exercises that focus on breathing, body-scan, yoga, or walking.

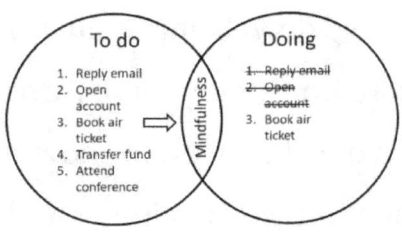

Fig. 3. Mindfulness do-list

One of the exercises that we can all practice with relative ease to incorporate mindfulness into our lives is to have intention.

Figure 3: This figure shows how you can list your intentions every day.

Mindfulness Exercise # 1: Intention

The first thing you should do every single morning is to have a clear understanding of what you want to achieve for the day.

As shown in Figure 3, draw two circles that intersect. Then, spend five minutes of your time writing down what you want to do for the day on the left circle. Once you've finished your list, you're now ready to start doing. As you begin each task, write that down in the right circle, being mindful of your intention on the task, how you intend on achieving the task, and the time in which you want to complete the task.

It is always recommended to give yourself a realistic time limit to achieve each task.

Once you're finished with a task, strike it off the list and move on to the next task. By doing so, you are setting a clear to-do-list for yourself. When you achieve every task, you will feel satisfied for the day. Whatever you have achieved that is not within the list is a bonus!

Chapter 14: What is Mindfulness?

Mindfulness is the capacity to perceive our thoughts, feelings, and sensations in their purest form. Acceptance plays a big role in mindfulness, whereby we allow ourselves to experience various thoughts and feelings without passing any judgment over them. The general spirit of mindfulness is rooted in Buddhist traditions, but the present-day form of mindfulness has been greatly influenced by Jon Kabat-Zinn and in particular his Mindfulness-Based Stress Reduction program which he created in 1979. Countless studies have been done since detailing the physical, mental, emotional, and spiritual health benefits of mindfulness.

Mindfulness allows us to recognize both our external and internal experiences, to be fully aware of who we are, where we are, how we are feeling, what we are doing, and not cave into distractions.

The following are a few things to note about mindfulness.

It is not obscure: Mindfulness is not something exotic that you have to become acclimatized to. It is something that should come quite naturally to human beings. Since the dawn of humanity, humans have been improving their lives through meditation and other mental training exercises. But in order to be successful in this pursuit, one must commit themselves.

You don't have to change: Most of the "solutions" that require us to change into different persons have failed us over and over again. Thankfully, mindfulness doesn't require us to become different people, but rather to maximize on our potential. Mindfulness exercises allow us to become the best we can be.

Anyone can do it: Most mental training exercises have been tailored for certain demographics but when it comes to mindfulness training, anyone can participate in this mental training program. All you have to do is observe the ground rules and stay committed to the program.

It's a way of living: Mindfulness meditation doesn't have a complicated approach that will take you to other dimensions of life. But it takes a simple and unified approach aimed at customizing your life experiences. The philosophy of mindfulness is simple — you can only improve your life by first fully recognizing your experiences.

It's evidence-based: Many studies have been performed into the efficiency of mindfulness and the results have been spectacular. The benefits of mindfulness meditation extend to the critical areas of life such as health, time management, setting goals, and achieving success. Mindfulness has been shown to help people become successful in all aspects.

It sparks innovation: As the complexities of life become more complex, we find ourselves needing more resources to surmount our challenges. Innovation plays a huge role in furnishing us with efficient resources and mindfulness meditation, an excellent mental training program boosts our capacity to innovate.

The great thing about mindfulness is that it doesn't cost you a penny. This cannot be said of most other mental training programs. Considering there are no economic barriers into mindfulness, everyone is welcome to start living this philosophy. The following are some of the general traits of mindfulness.

Nonjudgmental observation

Mindfulness meditation empowers a person to take on the role of the observer. This means a person should become fully aware of their thoughts, feelings, experiences, sensations, and people but not pass any judgment over them. When a person has mastered this capability, they are in a position to overcome their life challenges and become the best that they could ever be. Mindfulness teaches one to take on the role of the curious observer without presenting any form of a challenge too.

Acceptance

Most people who are battling against habit-driven challenges have one thing in common — an inability to accept their thoughts and feelings. For instance, if you have developed a bad habit such as ruminating, you can have a difficult time accepting that indeed you have been trapped into a bad habit and this causes you to avoid dealing with your problem. Mindfulness meditation teaches one not only to take on the role of the observer but to also accept what they see. If they see negativity and terrible thought patterns, they ought to accept them because it is in acceptance of one's limitations that one is inspired enough to take action to mitigate or eliminate their challenges.

Impartial watchfulness

Mindfulness encourages us to leave our biases behind. What happens when we are biased against something is that we end up having inaccurate perceptions and this takes away our power. We can become aware of our biases by being introspective and questioning our agendas. It really helps to be impartial as we watch our thoughts and experiences.

Present-moment awareness

Most people are trapped in ruminations about their past or future. These negative thinking patterns steal away their present. But mindfulness puts an emphasis on the present moment. A person must focus on recognizing how their present conditions affect them, as opposed to living in the past or anticipating the future, both of which make them susceptible to anxiety. When a person takes inspiration from their present thoughts and feelings and ignores their fears about the future, they stand a much better chance of achieving their goals.

Non-egocentric alertness

Most people have a hard time removing themselves from the equation. They find it hard to look at a situation without throwing in the "me" filter. But mindfulness empowers us to detach the self and become much more objective. Mindfulness advocates for a purely observational stance without throwing ourselves into the mix which is driven by our large egos.

Awareness of change

One of the goals of mindfulness is to help us realize the impermanence of our experiences. Mindfulness empowers us to take notice of the various mental and emotional states that we go through. It is not enough to just take on the role of the observer. Understanding that thought, feelings, and experiences are impermanent and are usually great motivators toward achieving goals. You become alive to the fact that you are not condemned to a certain unalterable state of being. Whether you are feeling happy, sad, anxious, or sorrowful, understand that it is a temporary feeling. Nothing lasts. Journaling will help you keep track of these changes.

Chapter 15: What is Mindfulness and What Are Its Benefits?

Mindfulness can be described as the state of being conscious of something or a situation. It can be said to be that mental state of concentrating one's awareness on the present moment. It also involves the individual accepting his or her present thoughts, feelings, and sensations, for the purpose of achieving a peaceful inner state of mind.

Mindfulness can be regarded as a long term therapeutic technique that heals the body, mind and soul, and it offers the following benefits;

#1: self-control and objectivity

People who are ruled by thoughts of their past mistakes and failures do not possess enough self-will or self-control that can liberate them from such past problems. When you achieve the power of now, you will learn to control your thoughts, which means you will become more objective and more rational in the way you think.

#2: Tolerance

It is very easy to spot people who are mindful of what they do- they are highly tolerant, not because they are weak, nor timid, they have mastered the act of accommodating people for who they are without judging them hastily. When you are mindful of a situation, you want to give people the benefit of doubt, and you don't just accept any belief someone else is trying to impose on you.

#3: Enhanced flexibility

Those who live in the moment are flexible enough to understand that their past errors should not determine future successes. They are opened to new ideas and new possibilities, and that is why they make each moment in the present count, towards achieving a greater goal and objective.

#4: Improved mental clarity

When you are mindful, you will be able to investigate every beliefs and thoughts and you only want to stick to the truth. People's opinions about you will always be bias because nobody knows you better than you do, hence you will consider all judgments passed on you are then find out which one is actually true and the ones that are based on other people's imagination or thoughts about you. Mental clarity is directly attached to improved concentration or enhanced focus.

#5: Drastic reduction of psychological and mental stress within a short period of time

Mindfulness is the most potent element to fighting stress in whatever form. According to researchers, mindfulness is the most potent power that can promote adaptive response to stress triggers. Another research indicates that mindfulness does not take the "avoidance" approach to problems, rather, it helps an individual develop a "coping" method through self-affirmation and visualization techniques of resolving problems.

Lack of sleep, low energy, agitation, irritability, and having difficulty in concentrating, are just few of the symptoms of stress and anxiety that meditation can help deal with effectively.

#6: Enhance cognitive powers and ability to deal with illnesses

Those who suffer from terminal illnesses can rely on the power of being mindful to cope with such. Mindfulness may not take away symptoms of chronic illnesses but can make such illnesses become more manageable. Mindfulness can help you induce a state of relaxation for the brain and the body as a whole- this will lead to better brain functioning, as well as increased in the strength of your immunity. With higher brain functioning, there will be increase in awareness, and ability to feel connected on any situation.

#7: Mindfulness speeds up recovery

Mindfulness will not only help you cope with an illness and enhance your brain power, it will also recover quickly from a life-threatening event. It can be extremely painful to cope with the loss of a loved one, especially a family member or colleague, but when you have developed the act of being mindful, your mind will speedily get over such losses or event. Post-traumatic stress is toxic development that must be dealt with at all cost, and the best way to go about it is to take complete control of your conscious and sub-conscious mind. When you are in charge of your own mind, you delete harmful thoughts and replace them with good memories.

#8: Improved academic performance

Adults are not the only ones who benefit from being mindful, high school and college students can boost their academic performance tremendously by eliminating distractions and taking complete control of their own minds. When a student starts practicing mindfulness techniques, he or she will begin to regulate their emotions much better, likewise, he or she will start to develop creativity and problem-solving skills- all these can combine together to enhance academic performance on the long run.

#9: Mindfulness boosts resilience and perseverance

There is no situation you can't survive if you persevere. The reason why we make mistakes continuously is because we don't take our time to study a situation before responding. Mindfulness will improve your emotional regulation as well as empathy, confidence, mood and self-esteem.

Resilience is a skill that will help you cope with daily struggles. There are mindfulness techniques that will be explained in subsequent chapters that will help you control your emotions (resilience).

Resilience can be a cognitive therapy that children can also learn.

#10: It improves workplace efficiencies

Mindfulness can make a huge impact on workplace performance. Being mindful in the work workplace means less mistake, more focus and more capabilities. As work-related stress is reduced, there are greater job satisfaction levels. Aside the enhanced work performance, mindfulness can increase productivity levels by reducing stress, fatigue and work-related depression- this means that more tasks can be completed within a short period of time.

There are countless other benefits one can derive from being mindful and living in the moment, all these hidden benefits will eventually show up as you continue to immerse yourself in mindfulness techniques.

Chapter 16: Mindfulness used in other anxiety related situations

When someone suffers from a specific diagnosed anxiety related issue such as those mentioned below, it is essential to try and target the matter in different ways. Having said that, the Mindfulness techniques that can be used in conjunction with whatever your doctor has prescribed – be it in the form of medication or actions – are the same. They are techniques that can and should be used always. Here are just a few examples of anxiety related situations:

Steps to help with Obsessive Compulsive Disorder (OCD):

Poor sleep makes Obsessive compulsive disorder worse. You need to get plenty of rest; a complete eight-hour sleep may seem like an impossible task to achieve but it is essential you focus on it. Make sure you are concentrated and focused on regular sleep patterns, getting plenty of fresh air, drinking a minimum of 1.5l of water a day to help eliminate toxins and replenish your body with the necessary fluids and also eat well.

Try to maintain a balance in your social life.

Stay away from alcohol as it contributes in large scale to mood changes, sleep disturbances and poor digestion.

Steps to help with Post-Traumatic Stress Disorder:

Try and be open with your family and friends about what is actually disturbing you or you can even discuss the same with a therapist. If you do not feel comfortable with talking, you can always write about your feelings and or the burdens you are carrying. Writing helps release tension and even if you are never going to read it again it's the doing so in the first place that counts. Writing and talking are both known to help raise your mood.

Stay away from alcohol as it contributes in large scale to mood changes, sleep disturbances and poor digestion.

Sunlight lifts your mood. so, get out there and get some sunshine for at least 15 minutes a day. This is also important to guarantee you get your daily Vitamin D requirements

Steps to help with Social Phobia:

Avoid alcohol, eat a healthy diet, get sufficient sleep and least 20 minutes of some sort of daily physical activity such as walking, running, rope jumping etc.

Try to spend some quality time with your friends or family.

Social Networking: Try to maintain a balance in your social life. Take up a hobby or sport that is not individual. This will help you socialize and meet new people. Let your friends and family know exactly what you are going through too so they can better understand your choice of words or attitudes at times.

Steps to help with Panic Disorder:

You need to take regular breaks from your duties and set aside some quality time for yourself to relax (have a bath, read a magazine, have a cup of tea etc). Try to live the moment and be committed to being present when you are with friends.

To cope with anxiety, smoking and drinking alcohol are considered to be a big no no. If you have these habits they will result in additional health problems which will consequently aggravate your panic attacks.

Learn how to manage your stress. The techniques referred to in this book are a great starting point for you. Also try other stress reducing methods as advanced meditation, progressive muscle relaxation, yoga or tai chi.

Chapter 17: Meditation

It is a good idea to create a space in your home where you meditate. This should have inspirational things placed into it, such as incense sticks, candles, flowers and items that you can contemplate while meditating. Remember that mindfulness meditation is all about using all of your senses, so things that encourage this use are good. Another thing to remember is that meditation can also be done in inspiring places. Perhaps you have a stretch of coastline near your home that is not crowded with people. Maybe you know of a hill that overlooks the country. The best things for your senses are those things that derive from nature. Thus, a woodland patch or a natural beauty spot will be perfect. As you will need to meditate daily, you do need to have that space in your home where you can go to get away from the humdrum of life.

Meditation helps you to explore your senses and free up all of the energy areas in your body. That's why it is done as a routine practice in yoga classes. In the case of mindfulness, it isn't to stop you from looking at things around you but is so that you can concentrate on them and use your senses to enjoy them, rather than having your mind wandering into the realm of difficulties and stresses. Meditation is excellent for good health and it will take you a while before you feel you are gaining from it. Thus, daily practice of meditation makes it more fruitful and something that you become accustomed to doing.

If you are unable to take up the Lotus position, which is where you bend your knees, seated on a cushion and cross your ankles, sit in a hard chair. Keep your feet grounded by having the whole of the soles of your feet in contact with the floor. Place your hands onto your lap palm upward with your strongest hand beneath your weakest. Thus, if you are left-handed, your left hand would hold your right hand or vice versa. As with the breathing exercises, you do need to be dressed in comfortable clothing. You can go barefoot if you wish and this is certainly preferable to having tight and uncomfortable shoes.

Start doing the breathing exercises that we taught you in an earlier chapter. Breathe in to the count of seven, feel the breath inside you and then breathe out to the count of eight. Do this until you feel that the rhythm is happening all on its own – remembering to use your nostrils for breathing in. When you feel that the flow is good and you are automatically keeping in the same rhythm, start to open your eyes and your senses and look straight ahead. Perhaps you see the flicker of a candle. Maybe you smell the aroma of incense sticks or flowers. Use all of your senses to be in that moment.

If you do find that any thoughts creep into your head, acknowledge them and then move on, dismissing the thought and going back to using your senses. You need to keep this practice up for about 20 minutes a day. You will find that it is exceptionally useful because it helps you to catch up with your busy life and to start it again with an added strength and vigor. At the end of your session, give yourself time to get back to normal breathing and movement because your heartbeat will have gone down and your blood pressure will have been lowered. Use this time to assess your meditation and to tell yourself what you would like to do next time that would improve your meditation.

Perhaps you would like more sensory items within view and can re-arrange your room before you meditate again. Maybe you need less because you found them to be too distracting. Use of this time to assess yourself helps your heart rate to come back to normal and then you will be able to get up and continue with your day.

Meditation in an inspirational place

I do encourage you to try this. Being close to a beauty spot or something that leaves your mind in a state of awe is an excellent experience. Sunsets at the beach or sunsets over the hills can remind you of how small you are in the order of things. You may wonder why people need to feel that small, but it's beneficial. It helps you to understand humility and to feel awe for everything that surrounds you. You need to tell yourself that even though you are small compared to what you see, you are an essential part of it all. The spirituality that you experience at feeling small will tell you that you are part of this scene and that without you, the scene would not be complete. It gives you a great sense of belonging and satisfaction if you can find a place like this to meditate in.

Remember to dismiss thoughts. Acknowledge them. Everyone has them but do not allow them to pull you into a chain of thought that takes you away from your meditation. Just dismiss them and move on. When you practice this observation of thoughts in a neutral way that shows absolutely no judgment, you find that you are much more able to do that when faced with everyday situations.

Conclusion

Being aware will allow you to live a better life and you will start appreciating the present more than ever. It can be quite difficult to find time for yourself, especially in today's world. This book will show you how you can make a better use of time and find peace within yourself. Being mindful simply means being aware of yourself and the ability to live in the present, without worrying about the future or thinking about the past.

By now, you will have realized the importance of being mindful. By being mindful of yourself, your surrounds, and others around you, you will be able to make the most of any given situation. You will be able to discover your true potential and you will definitely start living and experiencing your life like you are supposed to. You will be able to become more effective while performing your daily chores and you will be able to realize your true potential.

Being mindful isn't really that difficult. This book provided you with all the information that you need to know in order to start your journey towards becoming more mindful. So do yourself a favor and make a few changes… and you will surely start reaping all the benefits of being mindful.

www.ingramcontent.com/pod-product-compliance
Lightning Source LLC
Chambersburg PA
CBHW072003070526
44583CB00015B/1306